71 Different Healthy Habits

Keys to Happiness and Success

Shane Taylor

Copyright

© 2017 by Shane Taylor

All rights reserved. This book or any portion thereof may not be reproduced or used in any manner whatsoever without the express written permission of the publisher except for the use of brief quotations in a book review.

Table of Content

ABOUT THE BOOK 7

INTRODUCTION 9

ONE 10

1. DREAM BIG 11
2. STAY FOCUS 11
3. WAKE UP EARLY 11
4. EXERCISE 12
5. SAVE AND INVEST 12
6. BUDGET 13
7. PRACTICE GRATITUDE 13
8. THINK POSITIVE 14
9. LISTEN 14
10. SMILE 14

TWO 15

1. EAT BREAKFAST BEFORE YOU LEAVE HOME 16
2. GET AT LEAST 8 HOURS OF SLEEP 16
3. EXERCISE 16

4. CREATE A STUDY PLAN 17
5. STICK TO YOUR SCHEDULE 17
6. CREATE A CHART FOR YOUR ACTIVITIES 17
7. DETERMINE THE STUDY GOALS 17
8. BREAKDOWN YOUR BIG TASK INTO SMALL ONES 18
9. BE AT LEAST 10 MINUTES EARLY 18
10. TAKE A SHORT BREAK 19

THREE 20

1. BE YOURSELF 21
2. PLAN YOUR DAILY SCHEDULE 21
3. LOVE YOUR CHILDREN 22
4. LEARN TO FORGIVE YOURSELF 22
5. CARVING FOR PERFECTION 23
6. STAYING FOCUSED 23
7. HAVE A SUPPORT GROUP 24
8. TAKE TIME FOR YOURSELF 24

FOUR 26

1. START THE DAY WITH BREAKFAST 26
2. EAT REGULARLY 27
3. EXERCISE AT LEAST 30-45 MINUTES A DAY 27
4. EAT SLOWLY 28
5. EAT HEALTHY 29
6. AVOID LATE NIGHT SNACKING 29

7. Getting Enough Sleep 29
8. Eat plenty of fruits and vegetables 30
9. Hydration 30
10. Plan your meal 31

FIVE 33

1. Always show respect to your partner 34
2. Make a sweet gesture 35
3. Go walking with your partner 35
4. Turn off the television and spend time with your partner. 36
5. Express positive qualities about your partner to others ... 36
6. Reconnect throughout the day 37
7. Speak your partner's love language every single day 38
8. Express appreciation to your partner every day 38
9. Cooking and cleaning 39
10. Work together as a team 39
11. Spend quality of time in the morning 40
12. Snuggle in the mornings and evenings 40
13. Time Apart 41

SIX 42

1. Great Communicators 43
2. Credible 43
3. Problem Solvers 44
4. They have integrity 44

- 5. Assertive and Decisive 44
- 6. Have Humility 45
- 7. They are open to new ideas 45
- 8. Great Mentors 45
- 9. Supportive 46
- 10. Responsible 46

SEVEN 48

- 1. Automate Savings 49
- 2. Make a Budget List 49
- 3. Use Cash and Not Credit Card 50
- 4. Seek More Income Sources 50
- 5. Seek Advice from the Experts 51
- 6. Always Pay in Full 51
- 7. Conserve Energy 51
- 8. Prepare Your Food Instead of Buying 52
- 9. Don't Be Afraid To Say No 52
- 10. Live Below Your Means 52

CONCLUSION 54

ABOUT THE AUTHOR 55

About The Book

71 Different Healthy Habits: Keys to Happiness and Success covers various topics on how you can improve your life by exercising and establishing good and healthy habits.

In this book, you'll find seven different habits that can help you improve your daily life. Once you try to establish them into your life, your productivity will rise, and you'll be looking towards fulfilling all your goals in life.

Here is a Preview of What Topics to See Inside

- 10 Exceptional Habits That Will Significantly Improve Your Daily Life
- 10 Good Habits that a student Must Exercise
- 8 Habits to be a Successful Mom
- 10 Simple Habits that can help you with your Weight Loss Goals

- 13 Habits to become a Happy Couple
- 10 Habits to become an Effective Leader
- 10 Habits to Save Money

Introduction

Your Habits defines who you are. The person you are and the kind of lifestyle you have are all results of your habits. The habits that you have nurtured throughout the time will make or break you. It will dictate how fast or slowly you'll achieve your goals. So if you want to live a successful life, you must build good habits that will replace your current bad ones. If you fail to do this, you will not acquire the discipline, strength, positivity, and focus you need in achieving your desires and live the life that you truly want to live.

Since you've purchased this book, I'm assuming that you want to change or improve a portion of your life that is difficult to abolish or establish. I hope by reading this, you'll be able to find ways on how to start it and eventually adopt those that you've chosen to improve in your life to become successful in the future.

ONE

---

10 Exceptional Habits That Will Significantly Improve Your Daily Life

"When we strive to become better than we are, everything around us becomes better, too. " –
Paulo Coelho

No matter who you are or what you are sometimes, we find ourselves unsuccessful or not where we desire to be in our lives. For us to change our mindset, we often have to make changes to our habits and the actions that are causing us the problem. To help you with that, here are 10 exceptional habits that will improve your daily life.

1. Dream Big

This is the habit that you must always remember to do. You cannot succeed in life if you're going to underestimate yourself and the things that you can do. Whatever your plans are, always think beyond what you can imagine.

2. Stay Focus

Stick to your goals and don't get distracted by anything or anyone that will try to stop you from becoming successful. Also, staying focus means to do things one at a time to become effective. If you're going to do things simultaneously, you'll end up with unaccomplished results.

3. Wake Up Early

Getting up early is one of the common traits among most successful people as this dramatically increases productivity. Aside from the fact that this will greatly contribute to the accomplishment of your goals, it will also enable you to establish a beneficial balance in your life. By going to bed at a reasonable time and waking up early, you can bring balance to your life and enjoy the benefits of a greater level of concentration.

So if you're not a morning person, try to change your routine by setting your alarm clock back by 10 minutes on your first day to the first week. And then adjust it back by 15 minutes the following week. You may continue doing it until your body got used to waking up early in the morning.

4. Exercise

One of the best habits that a person should adopt is to exercise every single day as regular physical activity provides great benefits. Not only does it help you in staying healthy, but can also improve your mental health. Once the habit of exercising daily got established, you will no longer be tempted by excuses to delay what needs to be done.

5. Save and Invest

Your list of good habits won't be complete without one that calls for saving and investing. The truth is that, most of us were too busy living our present life that we forget the value of saving for our future. The more attention that you'll pay for this now, the more financial stability and success you'll get in the future.

6. Budget

The key to good money management is spending less than what you earn. This can only be accomplished by limiting yourself in buying unnecessary things. To help you with that, you must first identify each purchase and consider if it's in line with your personal goals. Otherwise, you may be spending too much or simply spending on the wrong things. Always make it a habit to prioritize the things that matters without spending more than what's on your budget.

7. Practice Gratitude

Cultivating gratitude is possibly one of the most effective habits in living a happier and fulfilled life. If you are thankful enough for even the smallest aspect of life, you'll be able to break free from any occasional pursuits that you may encounter. It will help you find joy and meaning in what you have and makes you less dependent on the achieving material belongings.

8. Think Positive

Always remember that positive thinking can help you gain positive results. This habit will help you boost your faith in overcoming any difficulties you're facing. Even more so, positive thinking can reduce stress and will help you improve your overall health.

9. Listen

Hearing refers to the sound that you hear, while listening requires more than that. The habit of good listening can greatly improve your career and is healthy for all your relationship. Effective listening entails observing the body language of the person you are talking to and noticing inconsistencies between their verbal and non-verbal messages.

10. Smile

When you smile, your muscles take a position on your brain that is connected with positive emotions such as joy and happiness. For this very reason, make it a habit to smile whether you're feeling happy or not to lift up your mood.

TWO

---

10 Good Habits that a student must exercise

"By constant self-discipline and self-control you can develop greatness of character"

Why other students become more successful than the others?

Although there are many possible reasons for this, it will certainly go down to one thing, and that is the habit that a student has. The student with a good habit will likely achieve success than the one with a negative habit. This is because the healthy habit will give the students the structure they need to attain their short or long term goals.

So to help you improve on your studies, I listed 10 good habits that you can practice every day.

1. Eat Breakfast before you leave home

Breakfast is the most important meal of the day because it gives you the nourishment and energy you need to endure whatever activities lay ahead.

2. Get at least 8 hours of Sleep

As a student, sleeping for at least 8 hours is very important as a bad sleep can leave you struggling all day. Good sleep can help you on being alert, staying focus both on your physical and mental health.

3. Exercise

This does not mean that you need to go to the Gym to exercise. It can be as simple as going for a brisk walk or jog with your friends. When you let your body get used to this, you'll find yourself more energetic and healthy than ever.

4. Create a Study Plan

Creating a study plan is a great idea to know what needs to prepare for your upcoming exam. This plan will not only help you to become organized, but it will also hold you responsible for the outcome of your own learning.

5. Stick To Your Schedule

Your study plan will not work if it is not followed with consistency. For this, you must try to make an effective study plan for you to follow for the length of the school year or semester. Always remember that sticking with the plan is very important.

6. Create A Chart For Your Activities

Creating a time chart will help you check on how to manage your time from day to day. Record all your activities like studying, watching, and even the time you consume when you sleep and eat. Try doing it for a week and see if it'll improve your time management.

7. Determine the Study Goals

Before the start of every school year or semester, try to determine why you need to study and what you want to accomplish in every class that you have. If you're planning to raise your grades on your classes, you need to start determining your study goals. For example, if you are preparing for an important exam in a couple of weeks to come, you must take the opportunity to grab your notes and start reviewing your previous lessons while you have spare time. Why? Because reading and preparing lectures ahead will reduce your future preparation time.

8. Breakdown Your Big Task Into Small Ones

A big task such as a thesis and reporting can be nerve-wracking. But if you try breaking them into 10-15 sessions per page, you'll find it much easier to accomplish. Try practicing this, and you'll eventually overcome the habit of procrastination.

9. Be At least 10 Minutes Early

Arriving early on your classes or appointments will protect you from any unwanted stress and problem. It will also give other people the signal that you are a responsible person and that you can be depended on. So make a good impression and always arrive as early as the given call time.

10. Take A Short Break

As a student, taking a break once in a while can help you maintain focus and can help you boost your performance in school. Once in a while, take your mind off of school and go for a walk or other things that can motivate you.

Always remember that change can't be done overnight. You have to motivate yourself day by day to be a better version of yourself. When you lose track on what to do in school, you can always go back on reading this book to be guided.

THREE

8 Habits to be a Successful Mom

"Successful mothers are not the ones that have never struggled, They are the ones that never give up, despite the struggles." – Sharon Jaynes

Most often than not, we see moms being troubled with a lot of household duties at home. Aside from taking care of the children, moms are also responsible for the house chores, the food to eat, and the well-being of the whole family. There are also moms that strive hard to earn a living but are still trying to maintain a perfect balance between their professional and personal life.

Being a mom is one of the difficult jobs that a woman can have since not everyone can handle the tedious responsibilities that a mom face every day. With this being said, I listed 10 healthy habits that will help you be a better mom than ever.

1. Be Yourself

Motherhood doesn't mean changing yourself or your identity. Motherhood is simply a phase in a woman's life where she'll start to be stronger than she has ever been. You don't have to succumb to the pressure and start losing your personality once you experience it, rather be yourself and enjoy the entire parenting experience coming your way. Your children will always look up to you and imitate what you do in your life, so it's good that while they are growing, they'll see how you'll manage to be yourself in every struggle you're going to face.

2. Plan Your Daily Schedule

One of the common mistakes that most moms make is that they don't plan their schedule in advance. Most of the successful moms take time in planning their schedule before every sunrise comes. Through this daily schedule, they don't skip important meetings or activities that can lead to disappointment for husbands and children.

Also, by structuring your work properly, you will realize that you'll be more productive in life. Not just that, planning beforehand will lessen the burden of having a lot of tasks all at one time.

3. Love Your Children

Your children need you now and will keep needing you until the end of time. This goes to show that you need to offer them your unconditional love no matter what happens. They say love is the strongest thread of any relationship, nurture it and do not be afraid in showing your kids how much you care and love them. Always remember that being expressive of your love for them will help them become good people in the future. Cuddle them around, kiss them and have that welcoming smile on your cheeks, each time you are communicating with them.

4. Learn to Forgive Yourself

Everyone makes mistakes, always remember that. I pointed that out for you not to dwell on your future mistakes on being a mom. There is no point in being obsessive about the mistakes that you have made or built up negative emotions that can make you feel guilty. Successful moms learn from their mistakes and move on in their lives. Trust yourself more and let your mistakes be a lesson for you on how to improve and get better in life.

5. Carving for Perfection

It's always a great feeling to achieve perfection in everything you do. However, you won't be able to hit your goal on everything that you'll plan to do. As I said, everyone makes mistakes. While your attempt should be towards perfection, you shouldn't be upset if things do not fall into place. Accepting that you can't be perfect on occasional times is a good habit that you must exercise.

6. Staying Focused

Nothing is as important as being focus when it comes to achieving success in life. This belief also applies when it comes to being a successful mother. You should learn how to stay away from all the distractions that may lead you to lose your goals. Time management also plays a big role in helping you stay focused in life. Keeping your schedule plan journal with you will help you on this one. By keeping track on all of your duties, you'll be able to finish all the activities you planned in just right amount of time.

7. Have a Support Group

Some of the successful people's secret to success is a support group that consists of friends, relatives, and family members. This support group can help you stay motivated, can reduce your stress and anxiety, and can offer valuable suggestions in difficult times.

8. Take Time for Yourself

Most of the moms tend to take their healthcare for granted because of their busy schedule. They also forgot to pursue their personal interests and stick with their day-to-day routines like cleaning, paying bills, preparing meals, etc. Before you know it, years have gone by. Try to make extra time in doing what you want like painting, dancing, baking, or knitting. It doesn't matter if you sign up for a course or try it on your own. What matters is you give time for yourself and in what makes you happy aside from your family.

These are just some of the healthy habits that you can practice to be a better mom than you already are. Once you get used to doing these, it will be easy for you to add more in the future.

FOUR

---

10 Simple Habits that can help you with your Weight Loss Goals

"It's not about losing the weight, it's about losing the lifestyle and mindset that got you there" -Steve Maraboli

1. Start the day with Breakfast

Breakfast is the most important meal of the day, and it's important in maintaining a healthy body weight. After an overnight rest, your body needs the fuel to get your metabolism working and provide energy for the rest of the day. By eating breakfast, you help your body boost your metabolism and reduce hunger throughout the day. Therefore it decreases the possibility of overeating and making wrong food choices for your afternoon meal. Also, people who eat breakfast regularly have better vitamin and mineral levels in their bodies.

2. Eat Regularly

Most healthy people believed that small, frequent meals are the way to go to lose weight. Why do they think so? Because when you go longer than 3 hours without eating, your levels of the stress hormone rises. When you eat small, frequent meals, the body becomes more efficient at keeping stress hormone levels low, which can help you not to eat more than what your body needs. Keep in mind that people who skip meals have the lower chance of losing weight.

3. Exercise at least 30-45 minutes a day

Exercise does not need to be vigorous to be effective. Consistency in exercising is more important than doing difficult workouts. Even regular light exercise will improve your mood and controls your appetite. Start with just 15 minutes of cardiovascular exercise twice to thrice a week, which can include activities like jogging, jump rope or a more gentle workout like brisk walking or swimming. Eventually, when your body got used to your workouts, you may add more strengthening exercises or training for even more health benefits.

4. Eat Slowly

If you're eating your meals hastily most of the time, you are probably overeating because of it. It takes a while for our brains to get the message that we're already full. So if we eat too quickly, we will actually eat more than what our body needs. Hence, the trick is to teach yourself to eat as slowly as possible. This is for you to feel fuller on a lesser amount of food.

One more trick is to eat a reasonable serving of food without consuming it seconds away after serving. A good rule of thumb is to use a moderate plate, and not to have food stacked up high. If you still feel a little hungry, wait for at least 20 minutes before you continue eating. By doing that, you'll feel that your hunger had already gone by that time.

5. Eat healthy

Try to eat healthy foods like fruits, veggies, and whole grains and avoid processed meat as much as possible. Whole, natural foods, such as apples, oatmeal, broccoli, and brown rice are low-density foods. These low-density foods take up a lot of room in your stomach as they contain lots of fiber, which are low-calorie ad good in satisfying your hunger. However, high-density foods or processed foods are the opposite. Examples of this are butter, oil, candy, and ice-cream. Eating mostly low-density foods can help you keep your weight in check without the feeling of depriving yourself.

6. Avoid late night snacking

Try your best to avoid surrendering to your midnight snack cravings, even if you feel the urge to munch on something. Try to go for a healthy alternative like nuts instead of chips and heavy meals.

7. Getting Enough Sleep

Researchers have found that people who sleep less than 7 hours per night are more likely to be overweight or obese. It is believed that a lack of sleep impacts the balance of hormones in the body that affects appetite. Not just that, not enough sleep can also cause deterioration in the quality of life that you have. So start adjusting your alarm and get enough sleep to achieve the healthy body that you want.

8. Eat plenty of fruits and vegetables

Most fruits and vegetables are high in fiber and are low in fat and calories, making them the perfect food when you want to lose weight. Fruits and vegetables also provide the body with essential vitamins, minerals, fiber, and other substances that are important for good health. The fiber in fruits and vegetables fill you up way more efficiently and also help you to keep fuller for longer hours.

9. Hydration

Water is one of the secrets that healthy people have since it has no calories and it fills you up while keeping your metabolism going. Start to increase your water intake now by keeping a water bottle with you at all times, or by having a jug of water in your fridge. If you find the taste of your water too bland and you can't take a lot of it, try to infuse it with slices of various fruits and vegetables, like cucumber and lemon, or lemon and orange to give your water a slight burst of flavor.

10. Plan your meal

Planning meals ahead is one of the ways to help you become effective in losing your weight. There are many reasons why. First, planning ahead keeps you aware of your eating habits and keeps you motivated towards your goal. Second, it's easier to follow through when you are not forced to make decisions in a short amount of time. Sometimes, we make unhealthy selections of food when we're hungry. So if you plan ahead, you'll be most likely to make right meal choices. Third, planning ahead ensures that your diet stays within the ideal calorie count that you just need to lose weight.

The habits we adopt can define who we are. If you are going to build a healthy habit and stick with them for long, it will become a routine, and surprisingly, the goal of being healthy will become more effortless. Habits tend to stick around for a long time and are usually hard to break once they got in your system, so if you were to successfully establish the habits above, you would be on your way to ensuring a lifetime, healthy lifestyle.

FIVE

13 Habits to Become a Happy Couple

"Every good relationship, especially marriage, is based on respect. If it's not based on respect, nothing that appears to be good will last very long." – Amy Grant

Every couple has a different way of establishing a healthy and romantic relationship. Some people are good on these things while some are having a hard time as developing a positive relationship is not easy. Below are some of the habits that you may practice to create and maintain a healthy and happy relationship.

1. Always show respect to your partner

Showing respect to your partner is a habit that is worth creating as it's a necessary component in creating a happy, healthy and long lasting relationship. When you express respect towards your partner, you are also expressing your love, acceptance, and warmth on them. When you express disrespect on the other hand, you are expressing that you don't accept who your partner are. Respecting your partner is all about giving value to them for who they are, including your differences. You may have a different outlook in life but this does not mean that you should disrespect your partner and put them down.

When you experience disagreements, try to make sure that you still respect your partner's differences. This does not allow you to humiliate and disrespect them out in public or in front of your friends and family. Always show how you respect them even on times of disagreement. There will be times where you don't agree on their decision but it will still be up to you on how you handle the issue on your differences.

2.   Make a sweet gesture

A simple gesture means a lot to your partner. If your partner likes to drink coffee in the morning, exercise this habit and express love through this act of service for them. Try waking up a few minutes earlier so that you and your partner can spend breakfast or coffee together before going to work. This is a simple yet powerful habits of happy a relationship.

3.   Go walking with your partner

If you love spending quality of time with your partner, make it a habit of going walking, either in the mornings before you start your day, or in the evenings before you sleep. This promotes conversation and quality time after a long day of work. Once you get used to this habit, your body will actually want to go walking. Walking with your partner also promotes good exercise that you both need. Before you start doing this habit, decide with your partner how long and how often you would do it a week. The important factor here is being on the same page and making sure that you make the mutual decision before establishing this habit.

4. Turn off the television and spend time with your partner

You cannot build a connection between the two of you if one of you, or both of you are constantly watching television. Make a mutual decision to turn off the TV and spend quality time together. Occasionally, you can cuddle and watch a movie, but try to avoid watching television in the morning or evening. Make some effort to ask your partner about their day and how they're doing. This habit will create a connection and love. Snuggle up while in bed or in the couch and talk with your partner. Talk about each other and what you can still improve on your relationship. There will always be something to talk about, whether it's your anniversary celebration or your next summer vacation. Stay focus on developing your relationship and talk about the things that need to be addressed.

5. Express positive qualities about your partner to others

The habit of expressing positive attributes about your partner will help deepen the relationship you have. On the contrary, expressing negative qualities about them will only build a wall between the two of you. This is a bad habit that eventually will eventually destroy your relationship. This negative form of behavior creates disconnection and lack of respect. Make it a habit of expressing the positive qualities of your partner to others. This positive behavior creates admiration, fondness, and love.

6. Reconnect throughout the day

We all have busy schedules every day that even connecting with our partner throughout the day is difficult. However, if you want to have a happy and long-lasting relationship, reconnecting with your partner throughout the day is important. This doesn't require you to be with hem the whole time; it can be as simple as sending a text or call during your break. This habit will keep the connection and focus that you and your partner have. Even if you have a busy schedule, you can still make the time to spend a text message or give your partner a phone call.

7. Speak your partner's love language every single day

Gary Chapman came up with a great book about the five love languages in which couples can express and experience their language of love and affection. Upon reading these five love languages, make sure to find out how you feel most loved and how your partner feels most love to help you stay connected.

8. Express appreciation to your partner every day

We often forget to let our partner know that we appreciate them. We think of it, but we always forget to show it. This doesn't mean that you'll have to buy expensive gifts to show your partner that you appreciate them. This can be as simple as leaving a love note before you go to work, cooking for them, making them coffee in the morning, or giving them a card. Make it a habit of showing appreciation to your partner every single day to maintain the quality of love you have for each other.

9. Cooking and cleaning

Cooking is fun, especially when you're with your partner. The habit of cooking together creates affection, connection, and love. Making, preparing, and eating food becomes an intimate act when you are with your partner. If you or your partner prefer doing the cooking, make it always a habit that the other person cleans the mess that was left in the sink or on the table. It is important that you always appreciate and value your partner, even if it's as simple as cleaning table or the dishes. It's always nice to know that your partner appreciates the love that you put in your cooking and wanting to do the cleaning is a sign of love and affection.

10. Work together as a team

A healthy relationship focuses on goals, either short-term or long-term goals. These goals are either for each or as a couple. Couples that are unhappy have nothing to look forward in life. They don't see each other as their long-term partner and are wasting time in making wrong decisions. To avoid this, focus on your relationship on creating, establishing and accomplishing goals. Happy couples have goals that can either be both small and big.

Follow this goal setting and start nurturing the connection with your partner.

11. Spend quality of time in the morning

It's easy to get into a routine in which you wake up, eat breakfast, go to work, come home, eat dinner, fall asleep and start all over again the next day. This routine definitely starts to bore your relationship and the connection that you have with your partner. We all have busy schedules that it's even more important to take time in the mornings and reflect with your partner. Try to focus on what brought you two together and appreciate that. It's easy to allow stress, frustration, and distractions to get in the way of having a happy relationship, but when you take the time in the mornings to love and appreciate your partner, you are establishing a habit that is filled with warmth, affection, and care.

12. Snuggle in the mornings and evenings

Take time to snuggle before going to bed and the morning after that. This can be as simple as holding each other in bed for a few minutes before starting your day.

13. Time Apart

Spending time together with your partner is very important as this keeps you both connected with each other. But just as important as spending time together is spending time apart. Being able to do your own things and remain independent is an essential part of your relationship. When you spend too much time together, one of you or both of you tends to be needy or dependent. This will eventually cause problems as you'll require more than what you both can give. Maintaining healthy boundaries and some independence will help you grow and establish a good and healthy relationship.

SIX

----

10 Habits of an Effective Leader

"Developing excellent communication skills is absolutely essential to effective leadership. The leader must be able to share knowledge and ideas to transmit a sense of urgency and enthusiasm to others. If a leader can't get a message across clearly and motivate others to act on it, then having a message doesn't even matter" – Gilbert Amelio

Leadership is one of the most undervalued but greatly needed skills in the entire world. It was opposite to what many people believe. However, leadership is not something you're born with; it's something you develop over time with a lot of hard work and dedication. The world's most successful people have spent a big part of their careers developing the leadership skills that are likely to bring success to them. Fortunately, anyone can build these successful habits if they have the will and desire. Read on these habits that most of the great leaders have and start doing them to succeed in whatever path you undertake.

1. Great Communicators

Effective leaders have a bigger, better vision for the company that they are in and articulate their vision clearly so that everybody is on the same page as them. Their planning begins with a clear vision of their desired direction and destination, starting with the objective and working backward to the present situation. They are well aware that achieving this goal means pushing people beyond their abilities and comfort zone.

2. Credible

Great leader models their work ethic. They are true to their words and show that they are one hundred percent committed to the task. They always inspire action by example. They organize their day in advance and strive to make the best use of their time as much as possible.

3. Problem Solvers

They don't allow difficulties to keep them from reaching their goals. They are able to think on their feet and think differently. They are not afraid to think outside of the box and ask 'what if.' They look at the obstacles as opportunities to grow and look at the situation from different angles. They take time in thinking and coming up with non-traditional ways to reach a goal.

4. They have integrity

Great leaders have inner values and are good in keeping true to their words, that is why people find it easy to trust them. They are dependable; they make promises and always keep them.

5. Assertive and Decisive

They have the ability to communicate clearly what is expected of people and won't take or accept any excuses. They make hard decisions even though it might make them disliked in that instance.

6. Have Humility

Effective leaders are not arrogant and boastful. They understand that they are no better or worse than others. They don't intimidate people. They know that success often comes from getting the most out of every single person in the team. They try to understand others and where they are coming from. Effective leaders also welcome constructive criticism and ask feedback from people they know they can trust.

7. They are open to new ideas

These leaders are always ready to listen with an open mind. They encourage creative thinking and believe that many minds working together can lead to success in every project they'll handle. They ask ideas from people and are able to listen without judgment.

8. Great Mentors

Successful leaders are ultimate learners. They don't just invest in the professional development of their department; they also invest in their own skills. They surround themselves with highly positive people and people that are smarter than they are, especially in areas that aren't their usual strengths. They certainly not pretend to know all the answers. They plan with others and are not afraid to work with executive coaches and other mentors for their own success.

9. Supportive

These leaders continuously guide their people through challenges and always find for solutions to foster long-term success. When you help employees come up with an improved work schedule to help them get through personal challenges like family or marriage, you're being supportive of both your employee and your organization.

10. Responsible

Leaders take responsibility for their actions and their people's performance. When things are going well, they make it sure to let their people know. When things require attention or if negative things arise, they find ways to fix things as quick as possible. When you can do this without burdening other people or blaming others to avoid taking responsibility yourself, you're being a responsible leader.

Remember that it's not always what you know but what you practice that will make you a great leader.

SEVEN

10 Habits to Earn Money

"Financial peace isn't acquisition of stuff. It's learning to live on less than you make, so you can give money back and have money to invest. You can't win until you do this." – Dave Ramsey

From learning a new skill every day to making your workouts regularly, habit takes away one thing that prevents us from getting things done and that is resistance. With good habits, we no longer resist -- we just do it.

You can quickly attain financial freedom by positively establishing the power of habit towards how you treat money. To help you with that, here are 10 habits that you can start to practice in order to save money.

1. Automate Savings

Automating savings is one of the best ways to save money. All you have to do is to set up direct deposit into a savings account through your salary, if possible. If not, set up an automatic transfer for a certain amount of money every pay period. If you never see your salary, you can't spend it. You'll still feel broke at the end of every pay period, but this way, you'll be broke with a savings account.

2. Make a Budget List

Getting on a written budget will help you save money as you'll be aware of exactly how much money is coming in and how much money is going out. Setting up a budget will help you allocate your money intentionally to each expense category, which will make you feel confident in spending the money on whatever it is you're spending it on. This way, you know where your money is going and can plan to save money.

3. Use Cash and Not Credit Card

One of the best ways I know how to save money is by avoiding using credit cards.

If you're a wise spender, using a credit card and paying it off regularly may worth really well for you. But if you are the complete opposite, and are close to being a shopaholic, I think this habit will be important to you. I highly recommend not giving yourself the temptation in buying unnecessary things.

4. Seek More Income Sources

The best way to improve your financial life is to earn extra income by maximizing your spare time or your rest day. You can start here by looking at areas where you can fill a need, or a job that requires a short amount of time or a flexible schedule.

Make converting your spare time into income opportunities a habit to help you earn more money for the future. You could freelance to anything that you're good at, or you can be of help to people with things they can't do themselves.

5. Seek Advice from the Experts

Develop a habit of seeking advice from the experts before making any major financial decision. This way, you'll avoid making any decision you'll end up regretting. When you make a habit of seeking financial advice, you'll be less likely to take financial risks that can cause problems to your savings.

6. Always Pay in Full

An extremely valuable habit that you need to master is to always pay cash and to never finance. The only exceptions are those necessary things like purchasing a home, paying for your children's education, or other important thing that you cannot be bought with cash. But for other things like home decors, clothes, or mobile devices, do not try to go on a payment plan. By getting on a payment plan, you're taking a risk that nothing about your finances will change. If you can't afford to pay cash now, then save up the money until you can afford it.

7. Conserve Energy

Make it a habit to always unplug your electronic devices that are not in use. Same goes for your other appliances like television, refrigerator, or air conditioner. You'll save a little money from it, but you'll see the difference when you constantly exercise doing it.

8. Prepare Your Food Instead of Buying

Getting in the habit of eating the food that you've prepared yourself can save you a lot of money. Try to avoid the temptation of buying food whether at work or at home by preparing your meals ahead of time.

9. Don't Be Afraid To Say No

One of the best habits that you can do for yourself is to learn how to say no without feeling bad about it. This doesn't always come naturally, so if you can't do it yet, try practicing it more. Practice makes it easier. Be open and honest with people especially your officemates and friends. Let them know that you'd love to go with them, but it's outside of your budget right now.

10. Live Below Your Means.

Many successful individuals mastered the habit of living below their means, even before they became extremely successful. This is one of the habits that you can add to your list in order to be successful in your goal of saving money.

Saving money takes time, it doesn't just happen overnight. Other millionaire took almost half of their lives to be what they are and what they have now. Start young because the younger you are, the more time you have to build wealth. That's only possible if you eliminate destructive money habits and adopt sound money habits.

Conclusion

Developing new habits need not be complicated. Just take one step at a time. The amount of time it takes to cultivate new habits will vary depending on how difficult it is and your willingness to make it happen. Your job is to pick one thing and take action. Just taking action is one step in improving oneself. You can do it!

About The Author

Shane Taylor is a content writer that provides uplifting content to help her readers develop their selves in all aspects of life. She hopes to inspire you and your family to become the better version of yourself by reading her books.

www.ingramcontent.com/pod-product-compliance
Lightning Source LLC
Chambersburg PA
CBHW050024230526
45470CB00003B/1117